Ode to the Unpraised

Stories and Lessons from Women I Know

Abena Beloved Green

Pottersfield Press,
Lawrencetown Beach, Nova Scotia, Canada

Library and Archives Canada Cataloguing in Publication

Title: Ode to the unpraised : stories and lessons from women I know / Abena Beloved Green.
Names: Green, Abena Beloved, author.
Description: Conversation, prose, and poems.
Identifiers: Canadiana (print) 20200279033 | Canadiana (ebook) 20200279084 | ISBN 9781989725214
    (softcover) | ISBN 9781989725221 (EPUB)
Classification: LCC PS8613.R426 O34 2020 | DDC C811/.6—dc23

Cover image: 123rf photo by Volodymyr Tverdokhlib

Cover design: Gail LeBlanc

Pottersfield Press gratefully acknowledges the financial support of the Government of Canada for our publishing activities. We also acknowledge the support of the Canada Council for the Arts and the Province of Nova Scotia which has assisted us to develop and promote our creative industries for the benefit of all Nova Scotians.

Pottersfield Press
248 Leslie Road
East Lawrencetown, Nova Scotia, Canada, B2Z 1T4
Website: www.PottersfieldPress.com
To order, phone 1-800-NIMBUS9 (1-800-646-2879) www.nimbus.ns.ca

Printed in Canada

For my grandmother,
Awo Yaa Baah Konadu

Contents

Introduction

When I saw the movie *Hidden Figures* in 2016, I couldn't believe that I was just now learning about these pivotal figures in the history of space exploration. How brilliant, intelligent, determined were these women! I was grateful that someone had finally taken the time to bring these stories to the big screen so we, the ignorant and eager, could witness and not only be inspired, but educated.

Ode to the Unpraised seeks to explore the practical knowledge, life lessons, and personal essence of everyday women through conversation, prose, and poetry. Many of these women don't hold professional titles and may not be interviewed or written about outside of this book. Their experiences and knowledge are valuable and their stories are humorous, informative, and insightful.

In writing *Ode to the Unpraised* I felt that I was on a mission to discover my own "hidden figures," some of whom I've known for years and others with whom I established meaningful connection through only a few conversations.

In my first book, *The Way We Hold On* (2018), the opening piece is called "This Life Can be a Poem." This second book is a demonstration of that. My goal was to draw forth the poetry from the lives and words of these twenty-six women. I hope that readers will find treasure in the anecdotes of these hidden figures and that perhaps they too will discover, in those around them, poetic gems of experience and insight.

For the women themselves, I hope you find contentment and fortitude in your own stories.

Background

In 2014, I wanted to interview my grandmother. She was a soft-spoken woman who married my grandfather when she was just fifteen. She told me that at this age, girls either continued their schooling or got married. It was the norm for most to marry and so she did. My grandma, Helena Baah Konadu, most commonly called Awo Yaa, was a wife and homemaker and, I'm told, a mediator and peacemaker in the family. I was curious about her entire life, from living in what was once Gold Coast, ruled by British colonialists, to how she felt about not being able to read English, to everything she knew about cooking. My cousin said our grandma never measured anything; she could tell how much of everything would make each meal turn out as it needed it. I wanted to know what it was like to be married so young. I wanted to know her thoughts and observations on any- and everything.

I planned to finally sit down and ask her all my questions after I completed my contract, in a different town in Ghana about five hours away. Days before the end of my contract, my Awo Yaa suffered a stroke. A day before I was able to fly from Accra to Kumasi to see her, she passed away.

After mourning my forever lost opportunity, I decided I could still speak to my remaining relatives even though I hadn't known them that well either. I realized, in fact, how important it was to do that – to remember them and learn from them in some way before they were gone. My idea then expanded to include my Canadian aunties, some of the first people my family met when we moved from Alberta to Nova Scotia in the early '90s. These women, though of a different race, culture, and geography, have become like family. After including the Canadian aunties, I decided to expand to other interesting women I'd encountered over the years and to include people younger in age as well. All of them are bursting with life experience and personality. It is a blessing to know and have spoken to all of them.

Process

Over the span of one year, from December 2018 to December 2019, I spoke with twenty-six women for this project. I asked them a series of questions on the themes of identity, family, life lessons, practical knowledge. As the conversations progressed, I added and removed some questions as I went along to tailor them to the individual, their context.

The women who shared their stories with me are located in various places. In Canada, they are in Antigonish and Halifax, Nova Scotia, and Toronto, Hamilton, and Belleville, Ontario. In Ghana, they are in Kumasi, Yonso, Abedwum, and Accra. Some of the women preferred to use only their first names.

I transcribed most of the conversations from record-ings of conversations. For a few – about three – I typed directly without recording them. The conversations that were carried out in Twi (a dialect of the Akan language) I transcribed partially in Twi and partially in English. It was a tedious process and, in the future, I would hope to hire a translator.

The poems in this book are written in a few ways: in my words as a response to the women's words; using mostly the women's words; and adapted from drafts of poems written prior that I thought aligned with the person or parts of our conversation.

There are many more women I would have liked to include in this book. Two of them passed away, while for others the timing did not make it possible this time. The absence of these people, many of whom are cherished friends, in no way indicates my lack of love and regard for them. Perhaps there will be a second edition and they will grace me with a conversation. To all of you whom I was unable to include in this book, I honour you too.

I: Bloodline

LaMeia

Photo by Mo Phung

LaMeia Reddick is from the township of North Preston, Nova Scotia. She is a creative and a storyteller whose career as a community engagement consultant has focused on bringing people together to have conversations, and to create projects and spaces that are inclusive and justice-focused. She is a multi-passionate artist who enjoys documenting memories through filmmaking, writing, photography, and movement. LaMeia thinks everyone should know how to grow food and find a way to enjoy a rainy day.

Healing Journey

My healing journey led me to writing love letters to my parents. Tears flowed as I spoke my words out loud. To my mom: I'm sorry and thank you. I realized I had been the hardest on her and that I was often taking her for granted. I was expecting her to be all about me. To my dad I said: I appreciate you and I forgive you.

For as long as I've been aware of them, my parents were not together. But there's this picture I look at of them and in it, I see that what they had was special for the time they had it and that having me was a beautiful thing for both of them. Their love was homegrown in North Preston. My dad was a DJ and ran the local community centre. He has a presence. He could have left North Preston and been huge if he had gone someplace like Toronto. My mom was nineteen when she got pregnant with me and that took her life in a particular direction. She can see my dad's face when she looks at me. Everyone can. Everywhere I went, people would say, "That's Puddy's daughter." No one would say, "That's Sondra's girl." I constantly had to say, "Yeah, that's my dad" and I identify as his but what did that even mean?

I grew up with a friend who had her dad around. The intimacy of their relationship is something I started to notice. He knew what she liked, her interests, her strengths. He'd bring her lunch to school. I see my brother's daughter climb all over him and slap his belly and laugh – it's amazing to watch. That physical connection between father and daughter. My dad and I hug but it sometimes feels distant. It feels polite. It's not an "I'm having a hard day, I need to sink into my dad's arms" kind of hug. I reflect on what it was like for everyone else in the community to have him to look up to but not to have him for me. I am the daughter of a legend who has given so much to the people and to everyone's kids but I wonder, was I selfish for wanting to have my dad to myself?

What is it about girls that grow up without fathers? I learned a pattern of behaviour where I expected the guy(s) I was dealing with to play a role that was not theirs to play. I wanted intense relationships at a young age. I always wanted there to be an "us," but not in a healthy way.

I will get there. We will get there. As I've gotten older, I've started to realize how similar me and my dad are. We have the same type of presence. Until now, I haven't been ready to face my dad and to say to him: *I've really missed you. I wanna see you, I wanna know you, I wanna understand you from who you were as a child until now. I want answers to some of those questions.*

At twenty-nine, I now have an opportunity to have a different type of relationship with my mom and dad. The recent passing of my grandmother, Myrna Loy Provo, changed the way I look at everything, especially how I view my parents. I feel a part of their evolution and I have compassion for their experience of learning to raise an adult. I know it's not easy and I'm so thankful for my wild family dynamics. I know I'm not the only one healing and grappling with these personal issues.

I'm trying to find out who LaMeia is and I'm discovering a new depth within myself every day. It's a constant journey that is fun and painful. I'm grateful to be aware of my life. I'm thankful that LaMeia Reddick lived. Isn't that something!

Love Letters

Homegrown love
child
sprung from a legend.
Puddy's daughter
Sondra's girl.
She notes the pattern
in their presence
and writes
love letters to each of them
F   U   L   L
of come-to-the-light
questions
and thank yous,
reflections
on how she came to be.
A daughter on a mission
always
a hand or two submerged
in paint
asphalt
flower pots
ocean
mental blueprints
that often come to fruition.
Popsicles in one hand,
surfboard in the other,
Luna at her side, sturdy and loyal,
she gathers her young tribe.
They are going to learn to ride waves
and film their
EVOLUTION.

BLxCKHOUSE Brave

"The best way to invest money is to buy property. My mom and I bought the house maybe six years ago now and the ownership piece has taken us to the next level. Me and my mom have a homestead. For someone like myself, I like to travel but having a place to come back to is important. Also, gentrification is real. If we lose our houses, we lose our communities, so owning our houses, our land, our space is key. Buy the hood. Buy the block. Let's be on our Nipsey Hussle.[1] That's where we boss up."

When your mom goes away for a few days, you and your younger sister get to work. You pull up the carpet and laminate floors. You paint the walls and put up baseboards. You inhaled copious amounts of dust, then hire a truck to take away the debris.

When you were fourteen years old, you read on a bumper sticker: "Get involved, the world is run by those who show up." You started showing up for community meetings, art classes, dance camps because, of course, you wanted to run the world.

At twenty-six, during a trip to DC, you saw the effects of wide-scale gentrification. You also saw young people fighting for what they believed – a city [Washington] that still reflected them; that they had a part in building. After this trip, you know you need to show up for your community, North Preston, stronger than before.

"Sorry, not sorry" becomes your slogan and you begin refining your vision. You begin digging for the right

---

1. Nipsey Hussle was Ermias Joseph Asghedo (1985-2019), an American rapper, entrepreneur, and activist who believed in community investment and upliftment. He was fatally shot in March 2019.

words to explain it. You go deep within to name it. Your vision isn't yet clear and you feel vulnerable in the process. Eventually, it emerges.

BLxCKHOUSE

A gathering place, a studio, a sanctuary. A healing centre, a holding place for kin and conversation. There is space here for everyone who leaned into your vision over the months. Its walls tingle with all of their energy. This is the space you wanted for Preston. A place that transformed within mere weeks. A space that continues to transform. This is the space you needed. This is the space you'd been looking for.

Liliona

Photo by Kinetic Studio_Kevin MacCormack

Liliona Quarmyne is a dance artist living in Kjipuktuk (Halifax, Nova Scotia) with her partner, Jon, and their two children. She is deeply proud of her children's ability to be their whole selves – their passion, creativity, and care for each other and the world. She believes it would be ideal if everyone could grow and raise their own food.

The Body Holds More Than Our Voices

A lot of Ghanaians living in Canada have a large group of Ghanaian friends. Filipinos often hang out with other Filipinos. That is not my experience. I don't have a cultural group of people within whom I can be guarded from criticism, misjudgement, or otherwise. I have to actively do that myself.

I had so much space growing up in newly independent Zimbabwe. The land I grew up on from ages six to eighteen was warm and vast. It gave so much room for exploration and vibrancy and hope. I didn't fit into categories in the same way that other people did. My passion was always in the performing arts and, in my circle, that was something that white kids did. Still, I had a supportive group of friends and my family fostered my ability to do all the things that I loved. In some ways not fitting in was liberating but looking back, there was a lot of bravery in my willingness to love the things that I loved.

I had this strong sense of self and often, others noticed before I did that I was the only person of colour in the room. I was often the only person of colour doing the things that I do. It almost doesn't make sense how I could know who I was with so many different influences and identities swirling around me all the time. I have a Ghanaian father, a Filipino mother, and we were part of the expat community in so many places. But rather than those being in conflict with one another, they were a cohesive whole. I never felt that I was choosing one part of myself over the other. I was able to hold all these pieces and to accept them as me.

Living in Nova Scotia has been making me smaller, less vibrant, less zany, less silly, less willing to speak my mind. More and more, I have had to accept the gap between people's perceptions of me and who I feel myself to be. People's misperceptions of me limit my freedom to move as I want to. I can't just have conversations with anyone. The tension ebbs and flows. The context of Nova Scotia makes it hard for things that are racially framed to get softer. I've had to work on not being small.

My dad gave me the best advice, not through words but through his actions. He worked constantly to be true to himself and to hold integrity. He is ninety years old and I still see him reflect on the decisions he's made in life; on whether those choices were true to who he was, is, and wants to be in the world. I find myself trying – sometimes succeeding and sometimes failing – to answer those same questions. My reactions and my choices: Are they true to me?

What I know is the body – moving, dancing, story, language, body wisdom. We live in a society that works to shut down body wisdom and sanitize it. The message is: *Dance is great, but it shouldn't look dangerous or wild or get threatening.* I've been blessed to have mentors like Diane Roberts, who validate me in trusting the wisdom of the body wisdom, in recognizing how powerful it is, and that it's okay to welcome and respect that power. What I know is that body is able to hold more than our voices can.

The Wind

What she knows is the dialect of body.
How the backbone is a reservoir for wisdom,
How the abdominals are the muscular
Scaffold both sturdy and swaying
The core that masters this motion.
She, a pastel rainbow gracing washed-out spaces
As if bringing promise after a flood.

Home changed its name like apparel:
Harare, Accra, Montreal, Antigonish, Halifax.
Zimbabwe was her first soil
Warm, vast, and vibrant.
Her childhood smile was constant.
She moved between atmosphere like water and wind.

She flowed like a garment,
Global tones adorning her aura,
Free from beginning, always explorer.
Bushes in new neighbourhoods
Brandish tiny thorns.
Once wind-free, her movement now cautious
Less vibrant
Less silly.
Her speech is tucked.

She found herself shrinking
In the flatness.

Her mother used to say don't settle in love
Or in how you live.
And her father showed her what it is
To look in the mirror and check your integrity.
What do people get, when they get you?

She reflects as her father did,
Determined to unshrink.

Are you still a child of the vibrant soil?
Are you still the wind?

Janelle

Photo by Janelle MacKay

Janelle MacKay is a singer-songwriter from New Glasgow, Nova Scotia, now living in Antigonish. She is the founder of Loomcast Audio. Two things that make her smile are her son, Mikey, and making music.

Concept of Being

I taught ESL in Halifax one time. It was a new experience, standing up in that teacher position. I never thought I could do that. That I would be able to command a room and actually give people something to learn. I've taught painting and songwriting workshops but those were intuitive to the person I was teaching. Teaching English was about rules and concepts. I had to have an impact. I always thought teachers were one of those pivotal professions – teachers, police officers. In kids' books these are the professions that are important. The students had respect for me. I had to rope them in a few times because they weren't paying attention or doing their work and they listened.

Going out and travelling on my own has also felt brave. I think it has to do with my upbringing. I wasn't supposed to be doing this kind of thing compared to what others around me did. It wasn't predicted. I had to change my relationship with fear in order to get anything done. It's been gradual. I still give a damn but less than before. Right now I have a coping mechanism: I cut myself off when I know I've thought too much and just go for it. That's on good days. I still have a lot of bad days.

Maritime Fruit

Hers is a strawberry heart
soaked in the musical heat of summer
where melodies are played beneath cricket wings
and between the swaying legs of long, long grass.

Hot strawberries send her back
to berry-stained tees and mouths.
Edible figurines
plump and squat
plucked and mashed
and made spreadable.

She was once like those little white flowers –
small, curious, unsuspecting.
And then, the harmony
and then – the reddening.

It's brilliant how it all comes together:
hot berries and organs
memories and music.
She creates her own chords
delighting in how we never run out of sounds.
The trained ones say: "That's not a chord."
She says, "But it sounds good, doesn't it?"

Dharmini

Courtesy of Dharmini Thirukumaran

Dharmini Thirukumaran is a multi-faceted entrepreneur, and a graphic and spatial designer. She describes herself as expressive, faithful, and trusting. She believes that everyone should learn how to tune into their Architect.

North and South of Sanity

I've had to change nearly everything about myself. Some things are rooted: my core joy, faith, being expressive and creative. Those are pieces of me that stay. But I've had to change everything else, including the thoughts that flow through my mind.

I used to view everything through my anxiety, trauma, and pain. I was very good at reading the room and constructing stories that I knew would make the audience comfortable. I knew my actual experience would bring discomfort to everyone. I wasn't ready to process their discomfort so I would just make up what made them feel good.

But that got taken away from me. I had to unpack all the things I bottled inside – or I would explode. God put things in my way to trigger the unpacking, to lay pain, shame, and suffering down. To someone who is full to the brim with these things, I say, let it out and don't fear being messy. It's going to get ugly. You're going to say things that will have people questioning your sanity and that's okay because sometimes you're going to slip in and out of sanity in that process. We live in such a bipolar society. The diagnosis of bipolar is handed out to human beings, but the earth is bipolar. There's north and south, there's day and night. It's just about how far on the spectrum you swing.

Don't be in your own way. Don't try to manicure it. Find people and spaces where you can unpack. Be messy but not with everybody.

Not by Sight

She grew up on a cashew farm
but used to hide under chairs;
violence and violations too big
to speak of without fear.

She did the un-doable:
left her home – two children in tow
taking nothing from the house
so no one would know
they were leaving.

Two new suitcases
filled with new things.
This is how you walk by faith
despite the storm twisting within.
This is how you lead your children to believe
in a God of survival.

She remembers sleeping on beds and floors;
strangers lending their roofs.
Her own house stands on the outskirts of town;
folks are always coming through.
Worlds away from the cashew farm
decades away from strangers' homes
she's a haven-maker
out from under the chair.

Her voice stays low and light.
She is feather and arrow.
Faith is her bow.
No place on earth is truly home
so she waits for direction.

No Breaking Away

My redemption involves the stripping of pride
the flushing out of judgement
the cleansing of spiritual pores.
My healing will come from honesty
and acceptance of repercussions
with the knowledge that no breaking away
will break me.

Michelle

Michelle lives in Eastern Ontario. She describes herself as reflective and resilient. She thinks people need to know how to do two things: one, listen to themselves and two, know how to calculate whether or not they're self-sustaining financially.

Set Sail

When you start making decisions for yourself you start to come alive.

Growing up things had happened as expected. I finished high school, went to university, and got married to my boyfriend from first year. My husband had a well-laid-out idea of what life would look like. There was no discussion about where we would live or how our life would look. We had kids. I stayed home and took care of them while he managed the finances. When I decided to leave my marriage, it meant I had to fend for myself for the first time. My kids and I ended up living with family for a few months until, finally, I told myself: *You've cried enough. You need to figure this out.*

First, I needed a job. I found one with a decent salary and benefits. When it was time to steer in another direction and do something closer to my heart, I found two new jobs. They paid less but I was happier and you know what I've learned about money? You can live on a lot less than you think and you can probably make more than you think if you're not so hung up on what you're doing.

I started speaking forth themes for the coming year. They started out based on how my life felt, not necessarily what I wanted, then they shifted to become intentions. The theme for that first year was rough seas. When things were really rough I pictured myself floating on water. You can't start swimming on rough seas – you have to wait it out a bit.

After I figured out how to make money, I had to find a place to live. I found an affordable two-bedroom apartment for my kids and I. Next, I had to figure out how much life was going to cost because I had no idea. I learned about utilities and about mortgages, how to save money on my phone plan, how to budget, and how to grocery shop within one. I made lists and looked at how the pieces fit. I got an app and set my food budget for $400 and nailed it. I didn't have money for Internet but we had a TV and the library had movies to borrow.

If you live in the ashes of your burnt-down house that's all you know. I learned that you can trust life. You have to put yourself out there and trust that it's going to work out. In Jamaica last winter, a local man said, "There are no problems, only situations." You could say a divorce is just a situation you need to figure out. You learn by being thrown off the dock into the water. You have to trust that it's going to work out. At the end of 2018 I set the theme for 2019 – "set roots." This was the year I was able to buy a house, a place for me and my kids to set down new roots for our life.

This has been the most challenging time of my life so far, but also the most rewarding. A lot of people drop out of your life when you get divorced, but I'm grateful for the people who stayed. I have healthy kids and a house that's warm. I can manage my home, my finances, and I have clarity. I've finally figured out who I am and now I get to live my life. I don't know whose life I was living before.

Chances

There are chances I have not taken
Lives I have not dared to walk in
Shoes in my closet
That I have not yet worn.

But this morning
I place my right foot
Into high-heeled leopard print
And tell myself,
"Walk and see what happens."

Messy

Dear Mama,
Here I am,
clean blouse
muddy soles.
Here I am,
avoiding the wrongs
you warned me about,
making
messy mistakes
of my own.

Manette

Courtesy of Manette Victor-Charles

Manette Victor-Charles was born in Port-au-Prince, Haiti. She grew up drinking papaya smoothies and today enjoys a sweet black cherry. When I asked her, "So who is Manette?" she told me of her challenges and new starts throughout her journey from Haiti to Canada. She has a degree in accounting sciences and studied at CDI College in Toronto and at St. Francis Xavier University in Antigonish, Nova Scotia, where she currently lives with her husband, Roland, and their two sons, Oliver and Sebastien.

What if You Just Play?

"Be flexible. Play! Even if the notes are not right."

My piano teacher reminded me that it's important to move. She said, "Manette, because you want to play well, you miss the point."

In Haiti, children used to pick on me because of my long hair. When I was twelve, I begged my mom to come with me but she said no, go by yourself. Stand your ground. My mother had ten children and a grade five education. She had a heart for justice and would have been a lawyer if she'd had the chance.

As an adult I am still summoning my courage. I remember sitting in the passenger seat of my friend's car as we sped along the 401. I shook my head: Could I ever navigate this anaconda of a highway by myself? Recently I was offered a job at the bank. I watched the other tellers slide cash quickly between their fingers and I thought, Will I be able to handle people's money like that? When I shared my doubts with my husband, he said, "Stop looking at your weaknesses. It will paralyze you."

All my life I've been a perfectionist. When I realized that, I wondered: Is this what has held me back for so long? I used to struggle to accept myself, but I'm too old for that. If I have to do something, I do it. If I make a mistake, I correct it. I faced the children who used to pick on me. I learned how to drive on the 401, and I know I can do the job at the bank. When my friends tell me that I am courageous, I take their word for it.

Taking Hold

I am twelve years old in Haiti
Ponytail, proper and prim.
The other children pick on me because of my long hair.
I beg my mother to come outside.
"Go by yourself," she says.
"Stand your ground."
Like a sword in timid hands,
I take hold of her words and hold them up:
"Leave me alone!" I bellow
And finally, finally, they do.

Toronto, Canada:
I sit in the passenger seat of my friend's car
As we speed along the 401.
Cars skim by like the rippling skin of a snake.
I shake my head:
Could it ever be me in the driver's seat
Navigating this anaconda of a highway?

I'm offered a job at the bank.
I watch the other tellers slide cash between their fingers
And I shrink.
Will I be able to maneuvre
With such speed and assurance?
My husband says,
Staring at my weaknesses will lead to paralysis.
Like an anchor in my shaking chest,
I take hold of his words
And recall my past successes.
And I accept the job.
And my mistakes

And my flaws.
And when my friends learn of my path
Across borders and promises
And tell me I'm courageous,
I take their words firm to my steadying heart
And I accept.

Esther

Courtesy of Esther Adjei

Esther Adjei is from Toronto, Ontario. She prefers cashews over almonds, pears over peaches, and, by the slimmest margin, mangos over avocados. She describes her younger self as curious, jovial, and smart. She is confident, kind, God-fearing, and loves to laugh.

Extra of Everything

I took myself out to a restaurant the other day. I wanted some of those fluffy pancakes. I told the waiter that my date stood me up. He brought me extra of everything and said, "Let me take a picture of you so your date sees what he's missing."

In the last five years, I've learned that you cannot constantly try to be please people – not your husband, not your family or friends. I was so invested in doing whatever it took for people to like me, I would overly extend myself, then feel bitter if the effort wasn't reciprocated. It took a betrayal for me to see that no matter how good you are to people, you cannot force them to value you.

I'm good at making people feel good about themselves. I appreciate that people like to be around me but at the same time, I can be a bit antisocial. I get invites then I'll make excuses. After a while people get tired of that. My friends say, "You're so flaky." I respond that it's okay, I just like my space. But now that I'm getting older and the invites aren't coming, I realize I need to stop that. Being a working mom of two, I sometimes miss the days when I had all the time in the world to do nothing and chill or hang out with friends.

I have a history of dealing with clinical depression and anxiety. Earlier this year I was praying that God would end my pain. I was tired of being depressed and felt like a horrible mother. I was so miserable that I thought my boys would be better off without me. I now look back and feel grateful for my growth, recovery, and newfound insights. I'm proud of myself as a mother. I'm not a perfect mother but I'm a good one. As a mother, no one can ever replace you. I cherish my life more than ever before and I don't think I will ever question my existence again. My love for my children overrides whatever trials and tribulations I face.

Forgive Yourself

Don't be so hard
On yourself
That you break.
Imagine forgiving yourself,
Making peace with your disasters.
No one could use what they know
As a weapon
If you cease the fire.
Walk differently
And move on.

Doing Hair

When I lived in Nigeria, my dad would drop me off at the hair kiosk on his way to work. I would sit and watch the skilled fingers cornrow, braid, and weave. I was three or four when I started practising on my own clients – long-haired Barbies my mom would send from Canada. By age seven I was doing real kids' hair. Their mothers would come for their appointments and bring their daughters to me so I could braid their hair for free.

When I got to Canada my mom had told every-one: *My daughter does hair.* After a whole day, the sixty or seventy dollars they would have paid elsewhere turned into ten or twenty. At sixteen I got a job at Tim Hortons. I made six dollars every hour, guaranteed. I quit braiding.

I started again when I moved to St. Catharines for

university. That's how I made my living for the longest time. I'm good at braiding hair. I make sure that the style suits the person's hair type and state. Then I consider their comfort. You have to make sure you're not doing it so tight they have to go home and take it out. Lastly, I put in my best. Even if I'm not happy that I'm doing your hair, I'll make sure I'm doing a good job because it represents me. Even if people couldn't pay a lot, I would give them quality.

Long Hair

Finally
Little black girl dream
Before afros
Were a style to look up to.
Dream comes true
Long after
She learns
Not to hang her happiness
There.

Afua

Photo by Historic Canada

Afua Cooper is from Toronto and lives in Halifax. She is a historian, author, and professor at Dalhousie University. Dr. Cooper is also a celebrated poet, who recently completed a term (2018-2020) as Halifax's Poet Laureate. Jamaica is her spiritual home. It's the one place no one can cast her out of. She feels everyone should know how to swim, ride a bike, cook, and drive.

The Triumph of Migration

When I was eight and a half I went from being the sixth child of nine (ten including our nephew who grew up with us) to being the only child. There was a wedding in my hometown of Westmoreland in rural Jamaica and family members had come from all over. One of my aunts who had come from Kingston fell in love with me and the feeling was mutual. Her son had moved out and so she was living alone. She asked my mom if I could go and live with her.

I appreciated the new attention I received as an only child for a while (later on, a cousin would come join my aunt and I). When you're one of many, your parents don't get to appreciate your gifts and talents. In Kingston I was exposed to a cosmopolitan lifestyle – more people and different ideas. I got to go to the movies every Saturday and living this freer life, I became adventurous. I also became the family historian. As a little kid I would go among the older people and ask them for stories. My grandmother used to tell a lot of stories and I would suck them up. Living in Kingston, I got to know another branch of the family living nearby in St. Thomas. As I got older and became more conscious of the mortality of the elders, I became more deliberate with my questions.

As an adult I've travelled all over Canada, to four or five countries in Africa, and to South America. I delayed my trip to Mexico for two years because my siblings would say things like "Oh my God, you can't go there! The cartel is gonna kidnap you." Finally, I went with my oldest daughter and didn't tell them I was going. Like me, a couple of my siblings moved to Ontario, but they never travelled outside of the province much. Maybe it's the trauma of migration.

Be Excellent

During my undergraduate degree, we had to read a unit on Frantz Fanon from his book *Black Skin, White Mask*. So many tings a me read. I didn't understand what the hell he was talking about. I wrote an essay on it and got a C minus. The professor said to me: "I know you're a good student because you always contribute to the class discussion, but this is not reflected in your paper." He gave it to me to write over. It went from a C minus to a C plus and I was happy. I'd been so careful; I'd read over the thing, took notes. It was a C plus but it felt like an A plus. After that I made a decision that I was going to do my best in every opportunity. Whatever you're doing, be excellent. Don't be in competition with anyone but yourself.

At the River by Sunrise

If you're not at the river
by sunrise,
she's gone.
The revolutionaries
had to be on the ball.
The event starts at seven.
We show up at eight-thirty.
If Harriet Tubman had been late,
do you know how many people
woulda still been in slavery?

Akosua Marfowaa

Courtesy of Akosua Marfowaa

Akosua Marfowaa worked as a trained teacher in Ghana before travelling to Canada to join her husband. She had three children before pursuing her university degree in nursing. She worked as a mental health nurse at St. Martha's Regional Hospital in Antigonish, Nova Scotia, for fifteen years, where she made many people feel seen and cared for. She is now retired and spending time with her grandchildren and taking care of her ninety-six-year-old father. She is Awo Yaa's only daughter.

Generations

When the water receded after the flood, my grandma took us to the riverbanks to see how far it had come up. I remember her singing:

Yɛ te ho ara yere twen Ɔnyame adom adom wura ei
Yɛ te ho ara yere twen Ɔnyame adom!

It says, "Hide me under your mighty wing. There's a big temptation that I cannot stand against on my own. So I need your help; I need your guidance."

My grandmother was a farmer. When my mom gave birth to my brother when I was around two years old, my grandmother came and took me to one of her farms. I remember the soup she would later make for my brother and I. I liked her laughter. Even though I was young, I never forgot it. I'd love the chance to sit and listen to her again.

* * *

My mom, Awo Yaa, sold anything and everything in the market – soap, cleaning powder, water, shoes. She also baked bread. Wherever she lived, in Juaben for instance, she would farm. We had plantain, cocoyam, yam, and cassava. The local people didn't like that she would sell her excess cassava. We were outsiders and they thought only locals should be selling, but that didn't deter Awo Yaa. You give her a small plot of land and she would put a garden in. She would sell a portion of the food or trade with someone else. There were lots of people around – children, grandpas, nieces, and nephews lived with us and there was always something to eat. Awo Yaa lived very simply. She wasn't envious of anyone's things. She used to say, "You can wear diamonds, I don't care." The simple life is what we were about.

* * *

I wasn't very good at housework. I didn't like cooking, especially not pounding fufuo. The pounding stick was so heavy. One way to get out of pounding fufuo was to go to the mill to make the bread. I would carry bag loads of flour, but I liked that over being at home. At home, all the girls had to eat together, but I couldn't chew fast so the other girls would always get more meat than I did. When you weren't there – if you've been sent to the mill, for example – you got to eat your own food at your own pace.

After helping my mom make bread I would go out and sell it. My mom liked that because I'm a people person and I always sold a lot. In my retirement, if I were to do something, I would maybe go back to have a shop by the roadside like my mom used to have. A store where I can sit with people and talk and laugh.

Arms

You wish
You could drink your grandma's soup
And listen to her sing again.
I wish
I had gotten there in time
To ask my grandma about her life.
Did she have time for introspection?
Or was it a more straightforward spell
Of creating, sustaining, bearing witness
To life and leaving
A humble memory?

You wish
You could listen to your grandma sing.
I wish
I could rub my cheek
Against the soft of my grandma's arm
Our love
More stillness than speaking
More wonder than knowing.
I wish
I had had my daughter in time
To meet her great-grandma.
But I believe baby girl
Met her
On her way to Earth.
Maybe one day she will
Join us in wishing for more time
With our grandmothers.
But right now
You are on this planet together.
You call her your travelling partner.
How lucky a girl.

Ɔkomfor Akosua

Courtesy of Abena Tuffour

Ɔkomfor Akosua Addae has been a medicine woman and priestess, an Ɔkomfor, in Yonso since 1979. She represents Frapo, the biggest spirit of the seventy-seven bodies of water in Yonso. She was given two choices: serve Frapo or go crazy. Though she knows she won't forget the knowledge given to her by the spirits, she agrees that it will be helpful for younger generations to write it down.

And the Spirit Came Upon Her

I didn't name myself. The elders came to get me in 1979. The water spirit – Nsuo Frapo – came upon me. It wasn't a dream *ooo*[1]. It wasn't a dream. The same way my mom was here, the spirit came upon me. I had just come from church and was pounding fufuo. My mom told me not to give in to it. She tried to break the spirit off of me for three years but it didn't work. You understand? I was given two choices, surrender or go crazy. So finally, my mom took me to Awonya, near Akyaia, for three years of training where I learned about the spirits and plant medicine. I've been working with Frapo from 1979 until now.

In terms of the sicknesses I cure, if someone wants a child, God blesses me to find the medicine for them to take. After about a month they are able to have children. Sometimes, the spirit will teach you about new medicines. You could be sleeping and they will tell you what to use for a certain problem. Every day, Spirit will teach you what to use for each sickness. Epilepsy, madness, medicine for marriage, travel.

I don't go too far for plants. I stay around my house. I walk around and look for what's close by. Ahahabia helps with jaundice. There are a lot of medicines. If we say them all you won't remember.

---

1. Ooo is an expression used to emphasize a statement or information you are giving.

Chosen

Her eyes sweep the ground,
Noting roadside remedies,
Downloading herbal prescriptions.

The spirits guide her:
This plant for epilepsy,
This for jaundice, madness, fertility.
A few yards away, a woman walks past
Holding an answered prayer.
Three months old, his curly hair flattened by sweat,
His fleshy cheek
Pressed to his mother's chest,
This child is evidence of a calling
Surrendered to.

The Ɔkomfor's voice is as soft as a footprint,
Her flesh, the colour of recent rust,
Her smile, easy,
Her laughter, like small bubbles,
Light and round, amused by all these questions.
Her fingers rest interlocked on her lap,
Careful extensions of the soft hands of a healer,
Hands that pray every morning for guidance.
You would think these hands and voice
Better suited for telling children's tales
Than for spiritual warfare.

No one can take her gift,
Though some have tried.
No one can seize her medicine,
Though now, with a bad knee,
The only thing she can't do
Is dance like she used to
When moved by the spirit.

Bloodline

I've been thinking about whether
I might have been a healer
If that's the type of thing that gets passed down
    generations
Like bracelets made of ceremonial gold;
Like advice on how to get a job or keep a home.

Most families aspired to raise a doctor, teacher, nurse, or
    engineer.
This great-aunt is a cross between doctor and priest.
At my grandmother's funeral
My mother points to the small woman sitting across the
    compound
Among the crowd of other family members.
She is toothless as a baby and never had any children
    herself.
I wonder if she couldn't have kids or
If she hadn't found a companion or
If love just hadn't worked out.
Maybe she didn't have time for a man
Because, like a nun, she was married to God.

I wondered if there was another blood route
This could have been passed down.
Whether, if I had been around,
I might have been the next healer.
I have always wanted to make people feel better
From the inside out.

II: Journey

Permission

In 2016 I asked friends on social media what they needed to give themselves permission to do. A number of them,
all women, shared. The following is a compilation of their
responses.

Permission

I give myself permission to be at home
wherever my feet are planted
for this particular time
for a season.
I give myself permission to uproot
to change my name
to change my mind
to fall out of love
to admit that I was never in it.
I give myself permission to seek my freedom
habitually, unrelentingly
and to find it.
I give myself permission to take up space
to be fat

to have no thigh gap
to love my body at every size
to keep trying
to pick up where I left off.
I give myself permission to question what I believe.
I give myself permission to believe.
I give myself permission
to give myself permission.

Barra

Photo by Julie Stinson

Barra MacNeil grew up in Montreal and lived in Alberta for fifteen years. She currently lives in Ohio, Nova Scotia. She has always enjoyed moving. Barra describes her younger self as energetic and impetuous. Two things she does every day are meditate for half an hour and read. She sews, knits, makes baskets, and loves cooking.

The World is a Miracle

My inspiration for living comes from an old friend. Enjoy your life, be grateful. I am trying to do that these days as I have had a most fortunate existence.

I always wanted to live on a farm. My friend Janie invited me to join her and family friends from Memphis who went camping every summer. I was eighteen. We spent a month in the mountains, living in tents. A couple years later, they asked me to cook at their ranch. That summer job turned into a year-round gig. That was the start of an era. I went from a private girls' school in Montreal to cooking on a ranch and feeding two hundred head of cows. Tunnel vision innocence to horseback explorations. We met second-generation old-timers, and saw how they lived. I don't know how I did all those things.

A wooden chair steadies her torso as she reclines, then leans in. She bends her knees and props her toes up in the slit between box spring and mattress.

I don't have the patience for book learning. My mother did. She would read cooking magazines and follow the specifics. I'm not good at following complicated recipes. I get constricted by what it's asking. I'm good at putting together leftovers; learning to assemble things that might go.

The walls of her bedroom are drenched in a mustard yellow. Woven baskets tumble over one another in the corner. One sits on the dark matte wood dresser that is nearly as tall as she is. Patterns etched. A fresh grey apron hangs from the silver lampstand. It is nearly complete. Red and white polka-dot fabric sits on her sewing table, lit and faded by the sun.

Friends and I started Goat Mountain School in the Kootenays for our kids. Once a week I taught children how to knit, felt, crochet, and weave little baskets. I stitched costumes and scenery for the plays. As a single parent the school was my family. It lasted seven years.

Family can end up spread apart. My daughter stayed west in Vancouver. My son came out east after me. He has a daughter now. So that adds to my being here in St. Josephs, on this farm. I guess home is the Ohio valley right now. And in terms of family it's my logical one that I take to heart. Life is changing all the time. That's the one truth we really know.

Her eyes are bright beneath eyebrows like small shrubs and amidst fine lines. She swipes bangs sideways on her forehead. Her roped glasses hang, leisurely lopsided against her orange checkered shirt. On her desk are eye-glasses, pads of paper, pink scarf, coral fashion belt, hand cream, deodorant, incense.

Sometimes we feel badly if we enjoy our lives because there's so many people whose lives aren't good. It's like, "Who are you to be happy?" But that whole guilt thing is so heavy. Put your regrets into context, learn from them. Put them to good use. I disappoint myself all the time for sure, but I have nothing to not be grateful for. The world is a miracle. Life is amazing as we know it.

Charisma

Courtesy of Charisma Grace

Charisma Grace is from Montego Bay, Jamaica, and lives in Halifax, Nova Scotia. She is becoming more strategic about how she loves and trusts. She believes that everyone should travel at least once to a place with a different culture, language, and people in order to live a more well-rounded life.

The Shape of Jamaica

My grandmother was the first person I loved. It wasn't until three years ago when I went to visit my cousins in Toronto that we began talking about growing up together in Jamaica that I remembered why.

It was a rainy day. I was between three and five years old and at home with my grandmother. My cousins and I were running all over the place playing hide-and-seek or some game like that. My grandmother was cooking in a coal pot, which sat on a tire rim – her makeshift stove – near the door. Even now I don't remember how the pot went off the stove. I must have tripped on it. The whole thing toppled over on my chest, burning me so severely that I passed out. People came, the neighbours, everybody. My cousins told me that everyone thought I was dead.

I was in and out of consciousness but do recall someone running with me in their arms up the road. The next thing I remember after being back home is my grandmother changing my dressings and washing my burns with warm water. Burns smell. Everyone in the house hated it. My younger cousins would say, "You smell so bad" and avoid me. My chest was exposed for weeks and in addition to the bad smell, it wasn't a pleasant sight. Still, my grandmother would dress me meticulously every day. She never flinched. Every day as she was dressing me I looked in her eyes and could feel her intent, energy, and commitment. I hated medicine so she would take one of the big capsules of antibiotics and open it onto the ripe banana for me to eat it. My grandmother nursed me back to health. Looking back, it was in that experience that I fell in love with her.

I only grew out of the scar in my late teen years. It was from shoulder to shoulder and my family members would say it looked like the map of Jamaica.

Risk

I didn't necessarily want to come to Canada. What I wanted was a better life, to study and to buy a house for my mom, my daughter, and me. I didn't see that happening in Jamaica so I explored options that would get me closer to my dream. I was working as a nurse and wanted to change careers. I was so disappointed the day I found out that I hadn't gotten the job I'd interviewed for. That very day, I started sending applications to every job I qualified for.

I saw an ad for Canada and thought, That's not going to happen. Who's going to Canada for an interview? I applied anyway. The job was for home care workers. Once you had a medical background you could apply. I thought it was a scam when the company responded a few days later. So I checked with the Labour department in my city and asked them if they knew anything about the company. I was sure these people were trying to trick me. Turns out, it was genuine. The interviewers came to Jamaica and the interview was right there at the Labour and Welfare Office.

I was overqualified, but they made promises to me that I could transfer my credentials towards further studies so I agreed to do it. Within four months, I had prepared and received everything I needed to leave Jamaica.

Still, I had not come on board in my entire being. I hadn't planned on leaving so I wasn't psychologically ready. I didn't know where the hell I was going or anybody there. I had travelled before but I had never been to

Canada. I didn't want to leave my country, my child, my mom. I was partially hoping they would say, "No, you don't have what we need."

The company had arranged an apartment for me on Bayer's Road and Joseph Howe Drive in Halifax, Nova Scotia. The apartment wasn't ready for us so we had to wait a month and stay somewhere else in the meantime. My first night was horrible and my first weeks were no better. I had to share my space with people I didn't know. I had to learn the bus route to get to work and I got lost all the time. Then it got cold with winter. I used to cry and tell my mom I wanted to come home. I had to constantly remind myself that I had made the right decision and try not to backstep.

Slowly I started meeting people. The gym became my sanctuary and I started looking forward to going as often as I could. It was a place that I could be lost in. For two hours of my day I wasn't off meditating on my circumstances, but being in a space where I could be free and unbothered.

There's no risk when you go after a dream. There's tremendous risk in playing it safe. The saying "You miss one hundred percent of the chances that you didn't take" resonates with me because while I never look at myself as playing it safe, if I don't see how something is beneficial I won't do it. I don't think life shows you the whole plan, though – we only see parts.

Meticulous Love

When the cooking pot toppled over
On her small girl chest
The burns left her unconscious.
The neighbours thought she was dead.
She recalls a relative running for help,
She in their arms bouncing.

Later, when her cousins would run from the smell,
Grandmother approached with warm water,
Washing her burns with meticulous love
And dressing her with unflinching fingers.
The same fingers would hide pills in ripe bananas
To make sure her baby healed all the way.
The scar dragged from shoulder to shoulder.
Family said it looked like the shape of Jamaica.

Decades later, she would leave the island
For better opportunities.
The scar had finally retreated
And the memory faded.
But the touch of meticulous love
Would run deeper and thicker than scar tissue.

Whole Peace

I want to be loved
as a whole
and live in peace.
Not loved as a hole
and live in pieces.

Akua

Courtesy of Akua Amoako-Tuffour

Akua Amoako-Tuffour believes that people should put the same effort into platonic relationships as they do into romantic ones. She loves cooking, planning, organizing, and dancing salsa. She is mother to a son and daughter and lives in Hamilton, Ontario.

Onward Web

"I wish you had learned the first time." This is what a family member said about the child I'm about to have. I spent a week trying to figure out how to process that comment. What was the benefit of making such a statement? Other relatives make comparisons: "Look at this person, she's twenty-six and married with four kids and her husband is a banker." Another called crying, asking what they did wrong to get this sort of behaviour.

Trying to manage the feelings of family members with my own is challenging. They don't mean any harm by it, I remind myself. *They're just speaking from how they see it.* When we are young our journey is part of our parents. As adults, we are on our own journeys running parallel. Sometimes family members see things from their own perspectives and project, insensitive to your needs and feelings. What I see is that nobody has it laid out. Nobody can tell you which steps to take.

In the past few months two people told me to be gentle with myself. Initially I was like *Yeah, yeah, I'll eat, I'll sleep,* without taking them too seriously. But it's been resonating in my mind. To be gentle with yourself means that even if you go wrong, you can be honest with yourself and still be compassionate. I'm compassionate with other people but I hold onto negative things about myself. So I'm learning to say, *Yeah, okay, you made a mistake. Yes, you're feeling sad right now, but you're also a great mother. You're sad but a great woman.*

Yesterday, I started to write again. I've been counting on God and returning to my faith. The best advice I've received is: You don't owe anyone an explanation. I don't need to satisfy anyone's ideas of where I should be in my life.

Reinvention

At the barbecue, you refused to eat
the beef hot dogs.
You were suddenly vegetarian.
And wanted us all to play along.

Deep and wide, deep and wide,
two functions of the fountain were you and I.
I deep with a few good friends,
you fluttering with many,
you butterfly.

You slipped identities on like costume wings,
absorbing Spanish like shea butter into your membranes.
You took up salsa, and instantly loved *my* favourite
      musicians.
I saw your shape-shifting as a mild deceit
while I was faithful to who I am.

It took me years to see the value in your transitions
but now I understand:
You were trying to create yourself
past shyness,
past small-town limits,
eldest child expectations,
adolescent insecurities,
towards possibilities,
toward foreign tongues
intertwined with yours in dorm rooms,
toward languages that felt palatable in your mouth.
Languages that made you feel
like you could have been born right here.

As the skin of your circumstances tightens,
you shift.
Seek terrain on the far side of "what if."

Sis, I *knew* you weren't a real vegetarian.
Months later, as easily as you had expelled meat from your
    diet,
you let it back in.

I'm the writer but you keep coming with the plot twists.
You call it "taking control of your narrative."
Brother is the engineer, and I'm a wordsmith
but you, you're a master at reinvention.

Catherine

Catherine lives in Northern Ontario. The places she has called home are her birthplace, Johannesburg, South Africa; Northeastern Ontario; Northwestern Ontario; and, most significantly, her husband, Condredge, who is Ojibway. She thinks everyone should know how to relate to people from different cultures in a respectful and authentic way.

Redemption

The best part of our wedding day was when we walked
    the aisle.
Back in each other's presence after morning preparations,
we restored each other's peace.

We called off the first wedding, six weeks to the date.
His addiction, active and exposed.
A wrenching confrontation. An inability to speak the truth.

I told him I need to think, knowing, devastatingly,
that I would return and pack for a more permanent
    leaving.

If he couldn't be honest with himself, then how
could we do this? Denial, no longer an option.
"Good enough" too weak of a base.

My brother, sister, and aunt fly in anyway
for what would have been the wedding week.
My humiliation dampened the whole visit.

The only thing more humbling than calling off the
        wedding
was breaking the news that he and I were back together.

When I picked him up after his treatment program
I felt it was the right thing to do
despite wondering: Am I descending back to denial?
Am I being ridiculous?
I felt that God was in it. So I drove
from the treatment centre in Northwestern Ontario,
to his home community to get his things,
then back to my town by ten p.m. the next day.
It was a twenty-hour trip.
The next morning, I started a new job.

I believe that love, in its ideal form,
strives towards redemption *at all times*.

When we asked the pastor to marry us, we described our
        journey
as one of redemption.

Responsibility

I

In the staff room, six or seven teachers discuss the Don Cherry fiasco. On a 2019 episode of his TV segment, the hockey coach was talking about people wearing poppies in Toronto, or rather not wearing them. He said, "You people love, you that come here, whatever it is, you love our way of life, you love our milk and honey. At least you could pay a couple of bucks for a poppy or something like that."

"He wasn't racist at all," he says. "He wasn't referring to immigrants, just people who don't wear poppies."

It's National Treaty Week and I'm excited to teach about it. As I begin with my class, they start spewing racist comments. Their words are similar to those made by one of the teachers in the staff room.

II

There was a church where Condredge and I used to go. An older gentleman would come up to him and say, "Hey, Chief." I used to volunteer to greet people at the door and Condredge would go find a spot for us. No one ever sat where he was sitting. If he sat in front, people would sit in the back. If he sat in the back, people would sit in the front. I'm embarrassed that I let that go on for a year.

I feel tongue-tied in these situations which occur so, so often. It's bizarre, how much I think about it. Maybe it's the people I follow on social media or because people do it poorly but I think, it shouldn't be white people who get to say, "No, that's not racist." At the same time I feel like it is something for white people to talk about because we have the responsibility.

76

Elizabeth

Courtesy of Elizabeth Glinz

Elizabeth Glinz describes her child self as an odd and naïve dreamer. She grew up in a small village called Forest Glen, outside of Truro, Nova Scotia. She adores her work at "The People's Place," the Antigonish Town and County Library in Antigonish, Nova Scotia. She believes everyone should know how to listen to each other without judgement and how to float on their backs.

Field Notes on Love

There's a Russian proverb that I sometimes think about that says, "Life is not like walking across a field." When I was young, I thought you fell in love just once and then you went on and lived your life in some sort of purposeful way. But I've been in love a few times and have had great experiences. I've been in love with wonderful people who I still care for dearly even though I'm glad we're no longer in a romantic partnership.

The first couple of times my relationships ended it was heartbreaking. I was in my late teens, early twenties. My sweetheart was a wonderful person. He loved art. He had taught himself and wanted to go study art in London, England. He wanted to be part of the art world there. I had really just started to figure out this whole responsible thing. I'd just gotten the job that finally felt like I'm doing a job that I think I could love in a community where I wanted to keep digging deep. I love the people; I just want to be here. I supported him being an artist but I didn't want to be part of that art world. He was trying to build a career and I was trying to build a community and home. So I said to him, "We just want different things here, don't we?"

It was a gift to have that revelation of what love could be. The same way that love isn't a fairy tale or as straightforward as walking across a field, love doesn't have to be bitter or turn to hatred when you figure out that it isn't serving us the way it used to. After parting ways with that first partner I learned that if it doesn't last forever, it's okay. It's heartbreaking but it always felt like the right decision. To end things is a decision of love, not rejection. It's honouring the person in front of you.

... But with Joy

I make music, not with any great skill but with joy.

I play ukulele the most, then guitar, the flute, and through the library I do a lot of sing-along activities. I also sing with the seniors' home, "The RK" [R.K. MacDonald Nursing Home], and then with the Sisters up at Bethany [Bethany Mother House]. I learned how to play the guitar as a teenager while doing Canada World Youth. I can play chords and get people singing songs they know the words to.

I'd been told I was a really bad singer, that I was tone deaf. I believed that for years until I played Ophelia in *Hamlet*. She had to sing. She didn't have to be good, but she had to sing nonetheless. I played the role and people told me my voice was beautiful. I thought, *What?* It was like the sky wasn't really blue! All this time I'd believed one thing and perhaps it was false. I've been singing ever since then.

I love getting other people to join in and seeing their joy once they get rid of their inhibitions and fear of failing. I tell them, "Isn't it great how much fun we can have together? We can enjoy each other so much when we make music." And when someone says they're not a good singer I say, "I don't believe you."

Ophelizabeth

You lent Ophelia your voice.
She lent you her name.
A fair enough exchange to break a spell.

You couldn't pull a tune
to Point B from Point A
even if the tune was on wheels,
they chided.

Maybe they weren't lying.
But maybe, with the passing of years,
your cochlea became finer
at tuning sound wave vibrations
into distinct designs.
Maybe your vocal folds were waiting
for
the right air pressure to fully unfurl
and demonstrate their musical skill.

And no one knew, not even you.

Or maybe
you could sing this whole time.
Ophelizabeth, careful whose critique you consume.
The wrong words might seal your lips,
have you believe it's better
that the air prefers its space
without your voice scratching up against it.

Let this be a lesson.
Curses in place of praise,
bruised words
up into which we grow

conscious or deaf of tone.
Sing, Ophelizabeth.
Don't believe everything
you hear.

Bernadette

Bernadette Arthur is a proud Afro-Caribbean Canadian who was born and raised in Scarborough, Ontario, but who is Trini to the bone. She loves exploring new restaurants that feature authentic cultural cuisine and being in the presence of majestic things like mountains, water, and forests. The owner of A Shared Table, Bernadette specializes in designing, curating, and facilitating transformational learning events that offer safe(r) space for people to listen, unpack, explore, create, and heal.

Everyone's Got Something Good

I'm good at teasing out who people are and what their gifts are. In some ways it comes out of the trope of being the "nurturing black woman." It's a trope that I know how to live out of as the oldest sister of five in a single-parent home. You learn how to make sure those around you are cared for and seen.

I've always wanted to see people. I could be sitting in an Uber and start asking questions that get to the heart of why the driver is doing what they are doing. If I have a sustained relationship with someone, I will call on them to do those things that I know bring them alive. I learned through an approach called asset-based community development that everyone has a strength, talent, and capability and that it's about pulling it forward. Everyone is an image-bearer of God and has dignity and worth.

Still, I deal with imposter syndrome. I wonder, What if I don't have enough experience to invite people into something like this? But I'm proud of myself for stretching. I literally choose these challenging situations and say, *This is a time to get some stretch marks.* It's uncomfortable as hell, but I'm proud of myself for trusting that I can do it. I don't say that enough.

See You

See you
See her
Make sure
She's ready
Little sister, run and play
Big sister, steady.
Brush and braid
Lead the way
Dinner on the table
Shoulders up, back, and down
Emotionally stable.

See you
See him
Make him a believer
Highlight all he has to give
Silence the deceivers.
He leans in, listens deep
Spine erecting straighter.
Candlelit reflection
In the image of Creator.

See you, see us
Orchestrated unions
Sequenced celebration
Innovational communion.

See you, seeing you
Momentary pause
Imposter syndrome
Lexicon
Hinting at your flaws.

See you, seeing them
Order from commotion
Justice over ignorance
Tenacious devotion.

Becoming One

Can't be easy
crashing
dreams.
Swallowing
conflict.
Microcosmic deaths,
grace to mollify flesh.
You cry and pray
and choose
to give,
knowing
the depth and width
of supply.
Lavished, we sit.
But human we cling,
co-dependant longing
for love to return,
bearing all the gifts we wished for,
already forgetting ...

Teresa

Courtesy of Teresa Turay

Teresa Turay describes herself as a playful, outgoing go-getter. She is a wife, mother to two young boys, and a nurse. The places she calls home are Sierra Leone and Antigonish, Nova Scotia. She is a strong woman who perserveres through challenges and fights for those she loves.

Unburied

The anxiety started in Toronto after I finished my first degree. I would smell gas in my apartment and wouldn't know where it was coming from. Once, I called the fire department. They came and inspected and said there was no gas and no reason to be scared. I started to wonder if it was all in my head. I started to become afraid of death and of losing control. I started to consider that it could be trauma from the war creeping in after all these years.

The war in Sierra Leone started in 1990 and ended in 2000. My sisters and I were there throughout. Our town, Makeni, was captured in 1998 by the Revolutionary United Front (RUF) rebels. There was no food coming in and you had to follow the rebels' rules. You would see people wearing your clothes but you couldn't say anything. The rebels burned people alive. They were the only ones with the food so girls would join them so that their families could get something to eat.

I used to make decisions and not understand why. I often second-guess myself and I always have a Plan B just in case my Plan A doesn't work out. People say, "T, you're always controlling." It's not because I don't want people to do things for me, but it's because I don't know if anyone else will do it. Whenever I'm at not fighting, it's as if I don't know how to live in a normal environment.

When my family arrived in Toronto after the war, friends suggested that we talk to a counsellor about what we had been through. We never did, though. Going for therapy is not something that's promoted in our culture. Now that we were safe in Canada we were expected to move on. Sometimes the mistake we make in the African community is that we try to bury trauma. We grow up, get married, start families, and then certain things start to come up. That is where I am. For twenty years those memories were buried and now I'm having to really deal with what happened.

My therapist asked me what I do to make myself feel good and I couldn't think of an answer. When I came to Canada new friends would ask me questions like "What's your favourite colour?" Having choices and favourite things wasn't part of my experience growing up. You wear what your mother brings to you. I grew up doing things because I had to do them. Now I'm trying to rediscover myself and what I really like. Lavender is my favourite colour right now. I've also discovered that I like nature and places where there is water. In Antigonish I like to go to the Landing Trail. Having favourite things is important. I want my son to know what he likes and to be able to make his own decisions. When you know what you like and do things you truly love, it can help you in a time of crisis.

When I got the news of my father dying, the first place I went to was the river in Chisholm Park. I knew that so many issues and emotions would come rushing in and that being by the water would calm me. My father spent so much time worrying about other people he never took the time to care for himself. When you die people will mourn for you for a year if you're lucky, but at the end of the day they move on. They love you but life doesn't stop. With all that came to the surface following my father's passing, I understand how important it is to take care of my mental health and start to deal with the issues that have been under the surface for so long.

How could you know

The memories wouldn't stay buried
After twenty years,
After moving away to safety,
After checking all these boxes:
Degrees, marriage, house, baby
You did it. You made it!
You've overcome.
Still, you smelled gas in your apartment
But the fireman said no cause for alarm.
You second-guess yourself;
You are calculating.
Always constructing Plan B.
You question whether your friends really like you for you
You wear an armoured attitude
As if you are still at war.

You had to follow the rebels' rules.
Girls would join them so their families could eat.
You would see random people wearing your clothes
But dared not say a word.
You could smell bodies burning ...

A steady state feels unnatural.
Peace feels uncertain.
Your sisters say "T, you're always controlling."

Your therapist asks what you do to make yourself feel
      good.
You can't think of an answer.
Growing up you did not have choices.
You did not have a favourite colour.
You did what you had to do.
You wore what your mother gave you.

You've checked the boxes and now, twenty years later,
It's time to check this last one
So that it doesn't destroy all you've worked for.
So you can stop fighting the language, friends, the
    memories.
You like nature and bodies of water
For now, lavender is your favourite colour.

Antoinette and Mary

Photo by Abena Tuffour

Antoinette Yeboah (left) and Mary Nkrumah (right) live in Akrokeri, Adanse North, Ghana, and are shown here with me and my cousin Steven. At the time of the interview in December 2018, Antoinette was seventeen years old. She loves English and Twi and would love to be a seamstress or nurse. Mary was twenty-two. She enjoys math and would like to be a seamstress. Both girls are mothers and work in the local mines. This informal mining is called galamsey. I met Mary and Antoinette while they were walking past the library on their way to work. They agreed to speak with us and we sat together on the library veranda and had a conversation.

Antoinette

Wiser

I do galamsey work to support myself. If they don't pay me, I don't get money to buy food.

I wasn't able to finish school, which is why I went into galamsey. My mother didn't have enough money to pay for me so by the time I was going to primary six, I was paying for myself. Some of the women would pay me to cook or fetch water for them. They would give me money and I would go to school. If I didn't get any, I would stay home. I couldn't sustain it.

My mom also goes to "gala." My father didn't take care of us.

I was really good in English and Twi. I wanted to be a nurse or a teacher. Teaching is hard but it's enjoyable and nursing, even wearing the uniform is nice. When I see my sisters as nurses, I like how they treat you and how they carry themselves. If I had been able to go to school I would have been really happy. I can read a little bit, maybe a sign that says, "Don't go here" but if it's really deep, I won't understand it well. If I hadn't gone to grade six, I wouldn't have been able to understand what I do.

If our mothers could have looked after us, we wouldn't go after men. At first, when we met guys we thought they were gods. We didn't think about family planning. My child's father travelled. Since he's been back, he hasn't been able to come and ask how the child is doing. Now I'm wiser. I've learned my lesson. The men don't help in looking after the kids. We, the mothers, have to look for something to do with our lives.

The work is hard. If you could see the rocks we crush ... it makes my knees hurt, but what makes me happy is that I can get up and take care of my child. I will work hard to take care of this one so that she can grow up and go to school. When she's older, she can take care of me.

false gods
(for Antoinette)

The men you once thought were walking gods
Turned out to be snakes in the garden.
Not bothering with promises anymore
They rarely check on their offspring.
You could have been a translator –
English into Twi and back again.
Could have been a nurse – white uniform
Starched and pleated pride.

You would greet young girls as you passed
Them on the path in the morning.
Tell them to meet you at the library
When the sun bows to evening.
You would introduce them to mathematical revelations
And penetrating philosophies.
You would teach them to read the signs
And understand the fine print.
You will be their evidence of what is possible
In the face of improbability
And in seeing you they will believe a better life is possible.
And as they walk back from the mines on the same path
    you once did
The young girls will see a new way forward
And denounce their false gods.

Mary

Still a Chance

When I get up, I go to galamsey. We carry their loads [the gold-bearing sand] from one place to the other and are paid afterwards. I have a three-year-old daughter who goes to school. I live with her father, but he hasn't married me. He said he would, but because of money, he hasn't.

I would tell a young girl in my position that she could be careful she doesn't have to do galamsey. She should focus on school. She should take whatever her parents give her – twenty pesewas even, take it. We are tired. We struggle before we eat. If someone gives me the money to go shopping for food, I will stop this work.

There are some kids that, because of the treatment from their parents, they will go to the boy's house and get pregnant. Then they are scared to tell their parents, so they will take some medicine to get rid of the baby and some of the girls die. Some parents don't take care of their kids. The kids are wearing clothes that are too small for them. Their uniforms are untidy. They go along with whatever their children are doing. If we can talk to the parents to watch their children, it will help teen pregnancy go down. Parents should have a meeting with nurses and the nurses can advise the parents on how to raise their children better.

I attended school until I was fifteen. My favourite subject was mathematics. I'd like to be a seamstress. Tailoring is a good profession. You can make a living for yourself.

Not God's Plan
(for Mary)

You can see it in her eyes
she's learned the hard way.
Twenty-two years old,
she is older than her age,
A model undiscovered,
a leader unknown.
Smooth ebony skin,
High cheekbones.

Her daddy taps palm wine trees
that he doesn't own.
He waits for weeks to be paid peanuts.
Her mother sells spirits
but the profits aren't enough.
Out of eleven, only one finished school.
He paid his way by carrying loads of sand
from one place to the other
in hopes that they contained fragments of gold.
And don't we all wish to pile enough fragments
to build a fortune?

"Many people die in this work," says Mary.
"But they aren't as strong as me."
She'd rather learn to sew and
she was good at mathematics.
She likes the sound of English
but she doesn't understand it.

Her child's father says he'll marry her
as soon as he gets money.
But he doesn't work right now.
If it weren't for her mother,
Mary and her daughter wouldn't eat.
"Galamsey wasn't God's plan for me.
But I'm doing it because I didn't listen."

She uses her money to take care of the baby.
Everyone knows,
it's the mother who buys the Pampers,
never the daddy.

III: Wisdom

Lindsay

Courtesy of Lindsay Burns

Lindsay Burns drinks coffee every day except for the days she's "violently ill." She calls enjoying her favourite beverage an almost sensual experience. Her favourite is Blue Mountain Coffee straight from the hills of Jamaica. The imported stuff doesn't taste the same. She is a clinical psychologist, and is passionate about music, drama, and politics.

Embracing Life as an Orchid

Through my training in psychology, I learned that some people are highly sensitive to their environments (like orchids) whereas others will thrive under almost any condition (like dandelions). My mother is a dandelion – bright and sunny, easygoing, unaffected by conditions. I was often inspired by her resilience and spent many years wondering why I couldn't just "get over things" like her. Then there was me – simultaneously feeling all my pains and the pains of the world, which left me frequently daunted by the discrepancy between the way things "should be" and the reality of what was possible. It was so easy to get lost in the minutiae of the forest that it was often hard to see the trees. At times, my idealism seriously got in the way of achieving my ideals – an orchid striving for perfect conditions that never arrived. Through the years, learning to embrace myself as an orchid instead of wondering why I can't just dandelion it up – only then did I finally learn to be the good gardener I needed myself to be.

Work It Out Theory

People say relationships are work. I don't really hold that mantra. If it was primarily a job, I would quit. It's funny because in psychology there are two philosophies. There are work it out theorists who say that any two people can build a relationship and do it with devotion. Then there are soulmate theorists who say it's about whether you connect; that here's a click and there's chemistry, a fit.

To be that absolute about it would be hard on either extreme. You'd be setting yourself up for disappointment in either regard. But honestly, you have to want each other first. I know there are many reasons why people hold on but I'm somebody who, if someone didn't want me, would rather they go and find someone that they did want. I think something really sad happens when people are with you but they don't want you.

Because I'm invested in someone and love them and actually care about their well-being and experiences, my respect, intrigue, and admiration is already there. So when challenges happen, I'll work it out because of that but I'm not going to work it out until it gets to that foundation.

Orchid

My mother is a dandelion
Sunny and unaffected.
I am an orchid
Sensitive to my environment
Struggling in all the world's imperfection.
For years
I wanted to get over things
Just like my mother.
To be in between any crack
And live to smile about it.

Seventeen

You and me and Ike
cross-legged on your linoleum bedroom floor
drinking tea,
whispering about trying weed,
laughing over strange lyrics,
like those in "The Gnome" by Pink Floyd.
Strange songs resonated with the strangeness in us.
We were our own first audience
in our attempts at poetic venturings.
Abstract thoughts we ourselves didn't understand
but they were edgy and perplexing.
The stranger, the more meaningful, we thought.
On the cusp of adulthood,
we were antennae
sending signals,
receptive to each other.
A bedroom floor huddle of discovery.

Two Old Men

Let's eat together in silence
Like two old men
Sit diagonally from each other
In the pizza shop after ten
Let's make it a tradition.
We'll come for the special
Cold cans and warm fries.
We'll have the whole place to ourselves.

Akua Gymfuaa

Courtesy of Akua Gymfuaa

Akua Gymfuaa is one of my grandmothers, also known as Nana Grace. Like most of the women in this family, she seems quiet yet opinionated, strong and calculating about what she needs to do; not stepping out of line but walking the narrow way to live a fruitful and faithful life. She is from Yonso, Asante Region, Ghana, and lives in Koforidua.

One Cup of Rice

I

"Ye fre me Akua Gymfuaa, me friri Yonso."

My name is Akua Gymfuaa, I'm from Yonso. I went to vocation school for a while. I like home management – sewing, cooking, and taking care of the home. I like cooking the best. If there are leftovers and different types of food, I can mix them and turn them into something new. Cooking doesn't bother me at all. I don't like when food is wasted. Everyone should know how to cook. Even if it's one cup of rice that you can make a meal out of.

If you work hard every day, God will bless you to put your hands to your mouth. But if you sit and fold your hands, you will find poverty. God exalts the humble and brings down the proud. Whenever I'm showing disrespect, I remember this and it keeps me humble.

II

We have to teach people in the community to see that everything God gave us, everything He did, we shouldn't spoil it. If we do, it's we who will suffer the consequences. It has changed a lot. Our water is spoiled and we've cut down so many plants and trees that erosion has started to occur. The foundations of our houses are being exposed and crumbling. We throw garbage everywhere and it's *basa*[1], *basa*, *basa*. We have spoiled it.

When the landowner comes, they will ask what happened because we are just the ones to look after the land. It is not ours.

---

1 Basa is a Twi word indicating that something is untidy or messy.

What happened?

Tongue bitten,
clenched eyes,
not all change is growth.
Water fogs, thickens
from infectious flow.
Slashed roots release soil.
The ground crumbles as
cement foundations sink.
Domino neglect.
Or is it lack of options?
Slash and burn the arms of oxygen
today too important to sacrifice for tomorrow.
This ochre ground is tired
of holding up houses
when promises keep breaking.
Dry skin shoulder shrug
exhaling on descent.
This is the new earth
unless we choose to ascend.

This isn't how the garden was left to us.
But by sweat of brow or any other means
we take what we can
and dream.

Auntie Kɔkɔ

Photo by Abena Tuffour

Auntie Kɔkɔ is also known as Atta Maame, meaning "mother of twins." She is a royal from the Oyoko Clan and her late uncle was Nana Asiama Aguashia Ababio II, the Chief of New Edubiase. She is on the finance and administration team of the Abedwum Development Committee. She has four sons.

A Word to the Young

My name is Auntie and I'm called Atta Maame. I live in Abedwum. I'm from the Oyoko clan, the ones who sit on the royal stool in Adanse Abedwum. If you say you're looking for Atta Maame, everyone will know who I am. Right now, because all the kids are not by my side, at first, I got tired but God had blessed me. I go to the farm every day. I walk six or seven miles there and back.

People, think of your future and where you are going. When we were in Obuasi, we saw that those who followed the mines and gold didn't get as far as they wanted. Right now, if you are a young boy or girl and doing galamsey, you can't get ahead. Everyone wants money, money, money, but it will get to a point where you can't do that work anymore. If you haven't gone to school or learned any other trade, you're stuck.

If you're a serious student, you could be a bank manager, doctor, anything. Someone could be a police officer, someone a solider, a banker, and other things that could help us. We could stand on our legs in Abedwum. Learning is very important to me and all families should let their children go to school.

I'm part of a committee and I want us to discuss what's working and what's not. We need to decide what we have and what we need. Now we have a library. We should get a community hospital. If we get a hospital or a community centre even, we'll be able to move ahead. This all stands on those of us who live here.

Young people, you're not behind in anything so don't rush to get money. Push yourself and work hard for your future. You won't have to depend on anyone, your mother or father. In fact, you'll help them. Be respectful. Be disciplined.

Auntie Kɔkɔ Says

Auntie Kɔkɔ says everyone wants quick money
but one day, the mines will wear you down.

She says those in Obuasi dig, sift, carry,
Bend, and wheeze, for passing payoffs
at the expense of lung and bones.
There's no future in it.

Besides, galamsey spoils the land.
You can't scoop the water and drink from your hands.
Some plants refuse to grow.

"Children, study hard," Auntie Kɔkɔ says.
Be a seamstress or a welder.
Build a community centre.
Help Abedwum stand on its legs.

Change rests on your shoulders.
Don't fear missing out.
Think of your one day, one day.
That's what Auntie Kɔkɔ says.

Nana Agyemang

Courtesy of Nana Agyemang

Nana Agyemang lives in Kumasi, Ghana, with her husband Yusif and their four children. She is a seamstress, entrepreneur, and homemaker. She is soft-spoken, focused, and believes that all people deserve respect, rich or poor.

Diligence

I'm serious about my work. I don't play with it. If I'm sewing, I do it well. If I'm selling something, I won't sell it and then "eat the money." You'll spoil your business if you do this. I'll keep the money to show for what I sold and put it back into the business. I've opened accounts for all of my children. At the end of the month, I'll divide it into four and everyone gets their portion. It's important to know the way you are doing the business.

There was a shop where I lived that was sitting there empty. One time it came to my mind that I had to do something so I started buying water sachets and selling them. I would get about fifty and would sell them within a week.

You have to know how to manage your house. You can't buy things randomly. Every day you go to market, but things you buy, the kids won't eat it. Learn how to manage what you have so you don't waste money *basa, basa, basa*. I learned from Awo Yaa. She didn't have money and her ways stuck with me. Sometimes, she could make us eat fufuo *saaaaaaa*[1] and sometimes we would ask if we could eat rice. She'd say, "When you grow up and go to your husband's house, you can do what you want." She made me see how the world is. Sometimes you will get what is sweet and sometimes you will get what isn't.

---

1 A Twi word used for emphasis, indicating that something is repeated or ongoing.

Advice to My Children

My daughters:
There are boys who want to
peel your skin away into gutters
taste you like an apple
toss you like the core.
They'll say they don't know you.
You
have to know
you.
You have to know
your future is full
of good things
worth stretching, waiting, working for.
Don't bloat yourself with false boldness.
Don't foolishly follow friends.
Don't do things that you wouldn't do
if you were sober-minded.
Some might tease you,
say, "This one, all he does is read."
"She's a goodie-goodie, too-know."
Stay on your path, no matter the names.
Your future is full of good things.

Awo Yaa's Fufuo

Awo Yaa didn't have money.
she stretched what she had like elastic.
She could make us eat fufuo *saaaaaaa*.
I told her other people eat rice some days.
Couldn't we do the same?
She said, "When you grow up and go to your husband's
    house,
you can do what you want."
Now, even if I have money,
I don't know how to spend it for fun.
I stretch it out like our daily fufuo,
pick small lumps so it lasts.
Awo Yaa made me see how the world is:
Sometimes you get what is sweet
sometimes you get what's not.
Either way, you eat.

Maleena

Maleena Imbeah studied at Achimota School and the University of Ghana, Legon. After her National Service in 1977, she went to Canada for post-graduate studies. Afterwards, she worked in Canada, Jamaica, Papua New Guinea, and Australia. She has two daughters. She is retired, living in Ghana once again, and loves working in her garden.

Plastic Activist

The men working on my house will drink water from that plastic bag and drop it on the ground in front of the bin. I have told them so many times to put their garbage in the bin and I've had to tell their bosses to tell them as well, but every time they come, I have to clean up after them.

Forty years ago, there was no such thing as plastic bags, and bottled and bagged water. We bought food wrapped in leaves or paper. At the market, we'd place tomatoes into our basket. Now, you go to the market and buy fish, they put it in plastic. They even boil kenkey in it. And of course, we dispose of it everywhere and there is little in place to stop this.

In the old days we were taught about hygienic practices around the home. You had to get up and sweep your yard and participate in community work. Town Council and sanitary inspectors would come around and inspect the villages and you'd better make sure your house was clean and that your water was covered. The inspectors would open your barrel and if they saw larvae in your water, they would fine you.

I don't think they do this anymore. We no longer have that cleaning culture. It's a shortcoming in the education system. I don't know who to talk to, but I'll talk to my classmates and we'll see what we can do. Maybe I'll become a plastic activist, who knows.

Parade

When I was young,
There were no plastic discards teasing our shins,
Or clinging, tattered, to bushes.
The water breathed easy.
So did we.

At the market, tomatoes rolled naked
And freely in woven cane baskets.
Banku and kenkey came hand-wrapped
In plantain leaves and paper. Hot and ready
To be swallowed and slide,
slide,
slide ...

Forward in time.
Today, crumpled plastic sachets lay
Discarded on roadsides
And at the base of well-intentioned bins,
Flattened, persistent.
Yet there are neighbourhoods
Where cleaners sweep tree-lined streets
As the sun is still warming on its ascent.

All over the city are graveyards
Of wrinkly black rubber,
Yolk-yellow jugs,
Brown, white, and pink ice-cream packs.
A cemetery that rises, as if on legs,
And parades through the streets.
And this is the first parade
I am sad to witness.

Kate

WOWPHOTOGRAPHYGH || 2019

Kate Amankwa, also called Sister Ama or Ma Kate, is from Asante Region, Abwaso. She currently lives in Abedwum, Asante Region, Ghana. What she's learned in life is this: "Life is not a race. You have to be patient. Also, you have to respect everyone. You also have to have the fear of God, read the Bible, and be a praying person."

Sankofa

Young people have money now, so schools need to teach students about money management. Schools also used to have classes teaching vocational skills such as how to make traditional meals – eto, aprapransah, kwen-kwen. They've stopped doing that but should continue it.

What we're giving up in our culture is language. Right now, in China, they speak their own language, but here in Ghana, they will say you don't understand English if you prefer to speak your own language. Our Twi language – we have thrown it away, so much so that when the kids come home from school, they speak English only. In Accra, you speak to someone in Twi and they look at you funny, as if they don't understand it. We have to hold on to our language, include it in our speech, and keep learning it in school.

Ɛse sɛ yɛ san kɔfa yɛn twi kasa no. Se deɛ yɛbɛtumi akyerɛ nkyirimma no.

* * *

It should be two people that watch children but their father died and left us seventeen years ago. We have four children, two girls and two boys. I sold the baked goods to look after them – chips, meat pies, and plantain chips. I also worked in the mines for a while. When I got a bit of money, I would pay the kids' school fees.

A woman named Sister Akua got me into selling oranges. We would sell them together at the junction along with my bags of pure water and homemade chips. I learned how to make chips while living in Obuasi with my husband when the kids were young. One of the girls who used to come to the house taught me. I stuck close to watch how it was done.

I've started sewing recently. When I was in school, I would cut shapes from paper, then take a needle and start sewing. No one offered to teach me the work I've learned to do. I stood and watched, and learned. As I stand here now, I can sew something for you without even taking your measurements.

Backs

We ride, tied to our mothers' backs
centred between her shoulder blades
aligned with her spine.
She is ocean and we rise
like the tide of our mothers' laps.

Our thighs hug the axis of her hips
tight in this cloth and snug we sit
just above her buttocks.
Who can harm us here?
What nightmares dare enter this haven
where I and my mother are one?

And our mothers, tied to us
by the cloth around her torso,
sell meat pies at the junction,
carry us on their backs to the farm,
lead us to the mines,
show us how to bend with a straight spine.
And though we work at their sides
instead of learning our alphabets
their love for us is no less.

Our mothers,
tied to us
by heart, by blood, invisible cords
tied by skin, strung
no matter the distance.
Do we bring you the same assurance?

Our plush bellies warming against your back.

Janie

Photo by Julie Stinson

Janie Humphreys is a farmer living in in Ohio, Nova Scotia.
She thinks something everyone should know how to do is
grow food and read. She says, "You can read a lot of junk
but it provides so much mobility and provides so much
pertinent information. It's what you read that counts but
you've got to be able to do that."

Amends

While studying psychology, I learned how a lot of things we don't like about ourselves we project onto other people. I realized that when I started getting in a rant about a quality about someone I didn't like, there was a good chance there was a part of myself that had that exact same thing that I didn't want to admit. I started to step back and look at myself, and at times realized I'm more of a jerk than I thought I was.

I'm still trying to work on myself.

I try not to be quick to judge and not to pigeonhole people or situations. I try to stay open and curious. I'd like to be more confident. I'm a severe dyslexic. I had dyslexia at a time when they couldn't diagnose it, so anything that involved reading and spelling, I was really put down by my teachers. But if it was math or sciences where I didn't have to read or spell or learn languages, then I excelled. I was very confused as to whether I was dumb or smart – that was the terminology used when I was growing up. I think that had a lot to do with my lack of confidence. I do try to live with my fears. Sometimes I'm not so good at it and I go, Okay, the time's not right. That's when you have another chance so you can approach your fears again with more gentleness and confidence.

Some of the best advice I've heard is to be aware of your habitual patterns and don't always succumb to them. It's so easy to revert to our patterns. Don't try to separate yourself from others, thinking, "I'm this way but you're that way." We are all inseparable and it's our ego that tries to separate us and also creates our suffering.

I feel that anybody can have a meditation practice. My practice gave me the opportunity to look at my mind in a non-judgemental way. Even though the judgement was always coming up, the practice was to not cling to those thoughts, to know that it was just thinking, and to make amends with myself.

Heaven and Earth

Producing food is how heaven and earth manifest themselves to nourish our bodies. As a gardener it's a privilege to be part of that. You have to hold the soil in your hand and get a sense of what it needs or doesn't need. The soil is key for that seed to pull the nutrients up from the earth.

You have to pay attention to frost. At night I cover my tomatoes, dark beans, and other crops with tarps, bedsheets, whatever I can use. The frost crystals on the plant act as a magnifying glass and burn the plants. If you can get up before the sun and spray the frost off, you can save the plants from being killed.

We talk to other gardeners and share information. It's a community so that makes it special. And you learn bits of science by being there. You can look at what are companion plants and arrange them in ways to support each other. You learn about the bugs that attach to them and when they come out and when they lay eggs. There are levels of understanding that you can go into or you can just give a song and a prayer and go to work.

You get some crops one year and the next year, it's a total flop. It all depends on rain. You know that you don't have the ultimate say in this and you're at the mercy of the elements. That's with all of life.

For my flowers I grow what likes me. For my vegetables I grow what will keep in my root cellar – carrots, potatoes, and onions. I like having fresh vegetables as a salad and so I can have cabbage, which keeps quite a bit. I grow things I can freeze, like spinach and corn. I can have the condiments that I want. I think of what I can preserve and I make the condiments I want. I try to grow as much food that I can keep over winter. I'm growing things I can take to Julie every time I go down to Halifax: peas because my granddaughter likes those, berries that are frozen, Swiss chard, corn. I grow a lot of beans for protein. You have to dry them after harvesting. You can hang them in the barn and they can stay there for a year.

Your grandmother and grandfather helped me. After they dried, they'd put them in a bag and your grandmother would walk on them. Then you throw them in the air and the skin comes off. I have a great picture of them. I brought a chair out for your grandmother to the garden and she would say do this or don't do that.

I loved when I had animals because I was using all their manure for the plants. Everything became interconnected. It just all flowed.

Ode to the Unpraised

To my great-aunt:
Whose name, mentioned once, did not implant itself into
    memory,
Who passed away without disruption or ceremony,
Who knew the science of soil, sky, and trees,
Whose skills were not hailed
but seen as ancestor worship. Witchcraft.
A practice to be shunned after Christian salvation.
We seek you.

To my great-aunt's daughter:
Who carries her mother's priestess occupation,
Who had no procession for her graduation,
Who will not be boasted of the way she may have been
if her credentials had been written on paper
if she were not consulting the elements and ancestors.
To women like you –
We see you.

For the women who can drain life from a sow,
midwife piglets into barnyard bassinets,
steward the death of a cow
with the same reverence offered to fresh-born calves
and do these things before breakfast;
Who are not strained by the blood of parting or arrival
yet are aghast to learn that you plan to walk down the
    aisle
on your wedding morning
holding artificial flowers;
For the women
Who will grow your bouquet from seed,
Who will literally turn the earth for you –
We sow.

For the women who chew flower petals like Pringles,
noting their spiciness, their suitability for salads;
Who make you recall when your schoolgirl-self
plucked purple clover petals and sucked their dainty
    straws,
discovering the sweetness hummingbirds hovered for.
For the women who collaborate with dirt and sun and
    roots,
Who model enterprise, community, and humility,
Who bake bannock on outdoor fires
while the frozen water holds us upright by the blades
as we circle on skates, making spectators of the forest –
For the women listen when you speak –
For you, we chew.

Acknowledgements

This book is an experiment in representing the voices of others authentically with an artistic spin. For encouraging, mentoring, and offering their time and services, I would like to thank the following people:

Anas Atakora, for your enthusiasm about this book when it was only a spark of an idea to actual words on paper first called Women I Know. Thank you for encouraging me to keep going and to trust that this is my place.

Lesley Choyce, for reaching out and giving my work a home at Pottersfield Press for the second time around. I am deeply grateful.

Julia Swan, for your careful reading and thoughtful feedback for this book and *The Way We Hold On*.

Peggy Amirault for your patient and precise work in laying out this book.

Olive Senior, my writing mentor from Humber School of Writers. Thank you for your attention to my words, your kindness, assurance, and honest feedback.

Mom and Dad, for arranging interviews and offering childcare and help with translations.

Steven Cobbinah for impeccably translating my questions and adding depth to the quality of my interviews in Abedwum.

Kwabena Danso, for using your voice to help me to gather this content from some of the elders in Yonso.

Paulo, for being there for me and Sey when so many of my waking hours went into this manuscript. Thank you for giving me the space, the hands, the time, and the patience. This would have been so much harder without you. Thank you from the bottom to the top.

All the women who bring these pages to life, for your time, your trust in this creative process, and your bravery. It is an honour to be your co-storyteller.

About the Author

Abena "Beloved Green" Tuffour is an award-winning poet, freelance writer, dancer, writing coach, and editor who seeks to create, engage, and elevate through words and movement. A first-generation Canadian, Abena grew up in Antigonish, Nova Scotia, and writes on various subjects that stem from observation, introspection, and an inclination toward empowerment. She has performed her poetry in Ghana, Ethiopia, Rwanda, and several Canadian locales. She won the 2016 Atlantic Writing Competition Poetry prize. She has a graduate certificate in Creative Writing from Humber College.

She has a spoken-word album, *Beloved*, that was released in 2014. Her first book, *The Way We Hold On*, was published by Pottersfield Press in 2018. Her poems address cultural, social, and environmental issues, relationships, and reflect on everyday life as a small-town raised, semi-nomadic, first-generation Canadian.